Strictly Cat Dancing

summersdale

Summersdale Publishers Ltd
46 West Street
Chichester
West Sussex
PO19 1RP
UK

www.summersdale.com

Printed and bound in China

All images © Shutterstock

ISBN: 978-1-84024-772-5

DISCLAIMER: *Strictly Cat Dancing* is inspired by the TV series *Strictly Come Dancing*, but is not endorsed by or in any other way connected with the television programme or franchise.

Substantial discounts on bulk quantities of Summersdale books are available to corporations, professional associations and other organisations. For details telephone Summersdale Publishers on (+44-1243-771107), fax (+44-1243-786300) or email (nicky@summersdale.com).

Strictly

Cat

Dancing

Felix Foxtrot

Strictly *Cat* Dancing!

Good evening, all you moggy movers! Here are your hosts: Jasper and the cat-ilicious Bess.

Bess: *Welcome everyone. We have a feast of dancing and prancing, glitter balls and fur balls – mamma meow! I'm just itching to find out which lucky felines are going whisker-to-whisker to win the Golden Furball Trophy in this season's Strictly Cat Dancing!*

Jasper: *Itching? I think you had better get a new flea collar, Bess!*

Bess: *HISSSSSS!*

LET'S MEET COUPLE NUMBER 1:
FIFI AND FELIX.

Fifi LeFluff is best known for her role in *Caternation Street* as Trixie, the loud-mouthed matriarch of the knickers factory. She's one moody minx!

Felix Diablo grew up in Spain and is a professional dancer. He was a finalist on last year's *Kitten's Got Talent.*

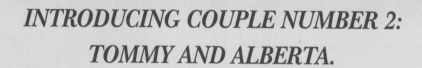

INTRODUCING COUPLE NUMBER 2:
TOMMY AND ALBERTA.

Star of TV's *Kittenia High*, **Tommy Pilchard** is guaranteed to set hearts a-flutter. 'Well, I'm just doing it for my old mum, who incidentally has a bad case of hairballs and… and I'm not sure she'll make it… please vote for me.' Aww, isn't he sweet?

Lady Alberta Brusque III may be heir to the throne, but she insists her dancing awards have come from hard work, blood, sweat and fleas. 'I'm not afraid to break a claw,' she yowled at our researchers. Me-ow!

Tommy

Alberta

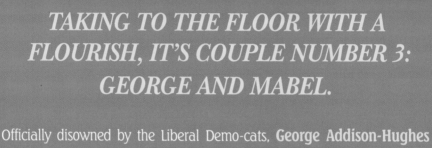

TAKING TO THE FLOOR WITH A FLOURISH, IT'S COUPLE NUMBER 3: GEORGE AND MABEL.

Officially disowned by the Liberal Demo-cats, **George Addison-Hughes** hopes his career change will get a kick-start here. 'Well, after my third wife left me, and my political career came to a halt, I felt the need to be surrounded by young, beautiful kittens again. Like Mabel here!'

Mabel Kotskovia was Russian Ballroom Kitten Champion between the ages of two and five. 'George has wined and dined me since we started rehearsing, I've put on so much weight, he 'as dropped me twice already!'

George

Mabel

AND LAST BUT NOT LEAST, IT'S COUPLE NUMBER 4: POPPY AND GASTON.

Poppy Allbright is an upcoming all-singing, all-dancing, all-perfect feline, with a solid background in the performing arts and celebrity cat parents. 'I just love to dance!' she exclaimed to our researchers, whilst trying to cat-wheel. And does she think her dance training will give her an unfair advantage in the competition? 'Oh, gosh no! I just want to bring a smile to the faces of all the little kittens. Kittens are our future!'

Gaston Noir – dancer, lover, secret agent – has starred in several movies about his own life. However, his specialist dance is the Lindy Hop. *C'est la vie!*

Poppy

Gaston

Dolores Batfisher is one sassy cat. A retired dancer, and now a successful singer-songwriter, she is best known for her stage-musical, *Mice!*, about the grubby rodents who live among the tunnels of the London Underground. *Mice! 2: Mice in Space* is scheduled to hit the West End next year.

Ken Meatyard may seem like an unlikely judge for a glamorous cat ballroom competition, but look behind the rabid stare and doggy breath and you'll find a true connoisseur of feline dance. Ken has written many volumes of contemporary poetry, including *Pad Softly, Sweet Kitten* and *Mewing Echoes of the Soul.*

Champion of Inter-Species Latin Ballroom five years running, **Lorenzo Bigglesworth** has made a name for himself on the controversial Human and Cat Dance circuit. Some say his motivation lies not in the sardines handed out by his human dance partner, Betty, but the large inheritance Lorenzo is set to receive upon her demise.

Sharpen your claws! **Nigel Clifford-King** isn't known as the cattiest tomcat in showbiz for nothing. With razor-sharp whiskers and the temperament of a queen on heat, some say Manx cat Nigel is simply making up for his lack of tail. Let's hope the cat's not got his tongue tonight!

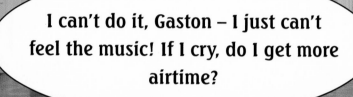

DON'T FORGET TO VOTE FOR YOUR FAVOURITE FELINE PAIR!

For Fifi & Felix
phone: 08000 123 000-1

For Tommy & Alberta
phone: 08000 123 000-2

**For George & Mabel
phone: 08000 123 000-3**

**For Poppy & Gaston
phone: 08000 123 000-4**

Vote lines are opened and closed at the times specified on the programme. Phone calls are charged at £7.60 per minute, mobiles may cost more. Votes taken after phone lines are closed will still be charged. *Strictly Cat Dancing* are not to be held responsible for bankruptcy, repossession, flea infestations, discoloured patches on the carpet, or the dismembered body parts of rodents left on your pillow.

FIFI AND FELIX'S FIRST DANCE – THE RUMBA

 3 It's like watching a whale seduce a prawn.

 5 Passionate, but her footwork lacks a certain elegance. *Diabolique!*

 **7** Who said prawn? I'm starving.

 **4** Shocking! I'd rather have salmonella than watch these two!

TOMMY AND ALBERTA'S FIRST DANCE - THE FOXTROT

Uh-oh! Tommy's well-groomed reflection is distracting him from the dance floor!

 10 Be still, my beating heart!

 5 Bunch of amateurs!

 2 Foxtrot? Hogwash!

 7 Stiffer than a dead mouse, but not as tasty.

  **3** This is a disgrace to cat-kind. Clodhopping corpulence!

 9 Mesmerising.

 **5** *Olé!* Or is it Oh-No?

 **3** Mabel looks like a glitterball! Time to lay off the kitekat!

POPPY AND GASTON'S FIRST DANCE – THE JIVE

The fur seems to be flying as Poppy and Gaston do the jitterbug!

Swing me by the tail!
I MUST win!

Poppy

Gaston

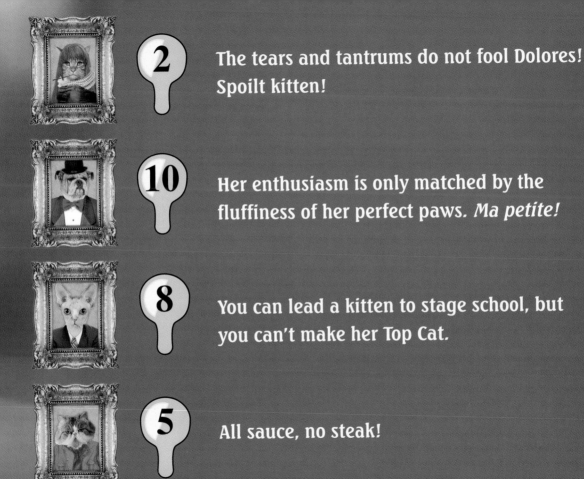

2 The tears and tantrums do not fool Dolores! Spoilt kitten!

10 Her enthusiasm is only matched by the fluffiness of her perfect paws. *Ma petite!*

8 You can lead a kitten to stage school, but you can't make her Top Cat.

5 All sauce, no steak!

BEHIND THE SCENES...

Bess: *So Fifi, do you think the judges liked your passionate performance?*

Fifi: I don't give a flying squirrel! I dance the way I live – dangerously!

Felix: I need a catnap.

FIRST VOTE-OFF

The audience votes are in... Whose footwork is a flop? Who definitely shouldn't give up their day job?

... The first to go is...

Fifi!

NO TIME TO ITCH, NO TIME TO SCRATCH; THE CATS ARE BACK IN THE STUDIO TO PREPARE FOR THEIR NEXT DANCE!

Bess

Each pair of cool cats has to work a prop into their semi-final routine. They need to show pawfect skills to make it through to the final.

BEHIND THE SCENES...

Bess: *So Tommy, how are you bearing up?*

Tommy: *Strictly Cats* has been life-changing for me. I hope my mother's watching. My mother is so special to me, even though I was part of a litter of twelve. I think I'm going to cry!

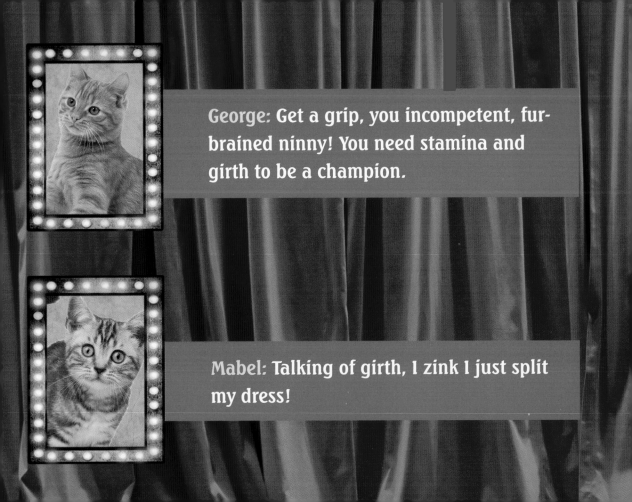

2 Get your paws off him, you lecherous old windbag!

 9 Their entangled friction is a poetry of passion. Bravo!

 3 This is not dance! This is an abomination!

 6 It's like watching a spider devour its prey!

GEORGE AND MABEL'S SECOND DANCE – THE VIENNESE WALTZ

George has chosen goldfish to keep Mabel's head up, turns out he can juggle more than his MP expenses!

George

Mabel

I'm gonna get you little fishy!

9

I don't believe it! I've never seen the lump of lard move so fast!

3

She resembles a vacuum cleaner; and I'm afraid of the vacuum cleaner!

8

Aye carumba!

8

She's big... but she's definitely not clever.

8 I see a new side to our prissy puss... And I am afraid!

10 A tortured tragedy of carnal desires. *Magnifique!*

5 Has Poppy's mind gone over the edge? The stresses of stardom!

4 The hamsters have more *je ne sais quoi!*

AND THE NEXT CAT TO LEAVE IS...

Bess: *The votes are in! Are you ready, dancers? I can reveal the poorest performing puss, the kitty with two left paws, the cat with absolutely no rhythm...*

Jasper: *... the cat who brings shame upon the species... Wait! What's up with George?*

It looks like poor George's nine lives are up. Poppy has made it through to the finals on a whisker! What

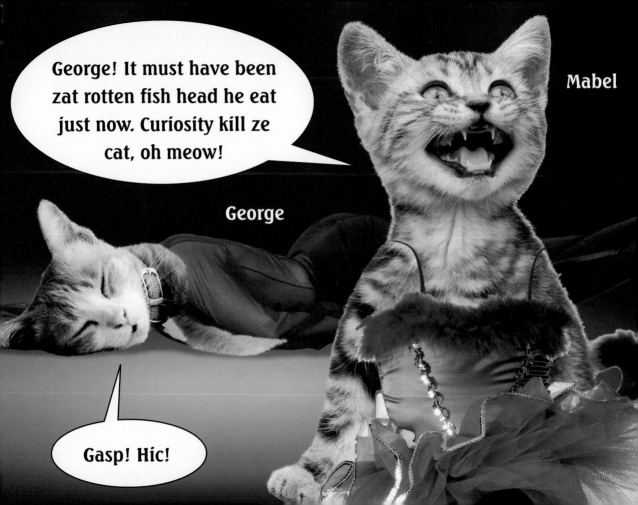

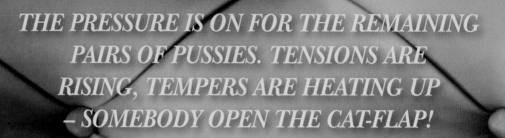

THE PRESSURE IS ON FOR THE REMAINING PAIRS OF PUSSIES. TENSIONS ARE RISING, TEMPERS ARE HEATING UP – SOMEBODY OPEN THE CAT-FLAP!

My fans may be ancient, but they've got pension to burn, my votes are through the roof! In your face, canary-breath!

Tommy

STRICTLY CAT DANCING : THE ALBUM

Calling all footloose felines! Now you can have all the thrills and excitement of showbiz without ever leaving your cat basket with the new *Strictly Cat Dancing* CD.

Featuring: 'Great Balls of Fur', 'Copa-cat-bana', 'Let's Face the Music and Moult', 'Eat a Tail Feather', 'I've Got You Under My Flea Collar', 'Come Spay With Me', 'Beyond the Flea', 'I Cat Rhythm', 'Lady Marmalade Tabby'.

So glamorous, you'll be coughing up glitterballs!

THE DAILY PURR

STRICTLY SCANDAL!

LOOK WHAT THE CAT DRAGGED IN!

Yes, *The Daily Purr* has let the cat out of the bag!

Rich kitty Miss Allbright was seen out rummaging for scraps in the alleys of Soho with none other than misunderstood mutt Ken Meatyard. Have the two found love over a portion of spare ribs?

Well, every dog has its day. Let's hope Miss Allbright's not just playing cat and mouse with his feelings – as we all know, canine Ken is a star judge on TV's popular *Strictly Cat Dancing*. Could Poppy be playing for points?

We say no cat about it! She's one crafty kitty.

Meanwhile, Mr Meatyard has nothing but kind words for his feline friend: 'Our love is a true Romeo and Juliet tale – we may be different species, but we share many interests: dance, the theatre, lamb shank.' And what about the *Strictly Cat* final? Will he keep his animal passions at bay when it comes to scoring Allbright's dance performance? 'Such monstrous allegations! I

should tear you a new tail! GRRRRR!'

Yikes! Sensitive for a big bruiser, isn't he? We at *The Daily Purr* wish the interspecies couple the very best, and hope they will consider our six-figure offer for exclusive rights to the wedding coverage.

OUR PRESENTERS INTRODUCE THE FINAL

Jasper: *It's the final dance of the series! My fur is on end!*

Bess: *All right Jasper, don't drop your false teeth. Yes, it's the moment we have been waiting for! Let's take a look behind the scenes.*

Alberta

I feel pretty,
Oh so pretty!

FINAL PREPARATIONS

In the furry frenzy of the final preparations nobody notices Poppy secretly spike Alberta's skimmed milk with triple-strength catnip. What a back-pawed move!

FINAL PREPARATIONS

Tommy can charm the whiskers off a cat!
Even Dolores is grinning like a Cheshire
when Tommy purrs by.

Dolores

Oh Tom, you do know how to make an old cat feel like a spring-kitten again.

JUDGES' PREDICTIONS…

What do our critics want to see from our pussy pairs tonight? Are they cat dancers or ballroom chancers?

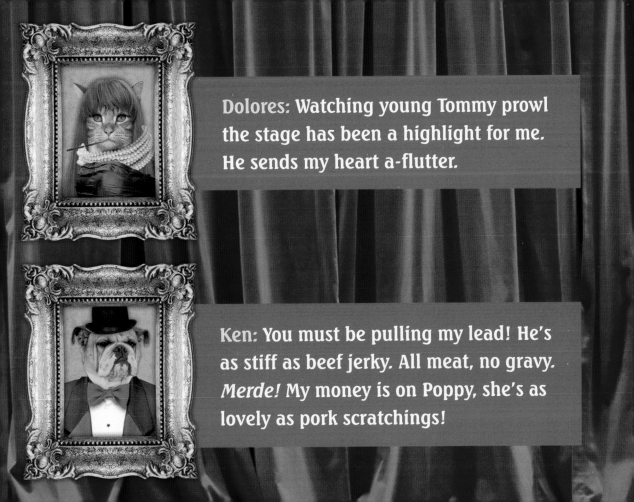

Dolores: Watching young Tommy prowl the stage has been a highlight for me. He sends my heart a-flutter.

Ken: You must be pulling my lead! He's as stiff as beef jerky. All meat, no gravy. *Merde!* My money is on Poppy, she's as lovely as pork scratchings!

Lorenzo: Ken is away with the fairies, Poppy has turned his head! I will tango up the M1 before that powder puff gets her claws on the trophy. And Tommy cannot salsa to save his hide. It's Cat 22!

Nigel: I've seen better standards of dance when my cousin had a bad case of worms. Though I must say, Tommy does have style.

*SOMEBODY NEUTER THESE WILDCATS!
THE CHANCES SEEM FIFTY-FIFTY, BUT
SOMEONE HAS TO BE STRICTLY CAT
CHAMPION. OH PURRLEASE, WE'VE WAITED
LONG ENOUGH, ON WITH THE SHOW!*

 3

A-paw-ling!

10

Poppy can move faster than a Siamese on skates! Bravo!

 4

The flashiest piece of codswallop I've ever seen.

2

I'm surprised the crocodile tears do not extinguish the sparklers.

OUR PRESENTERS INTRODUCE THE FINAL DANCE

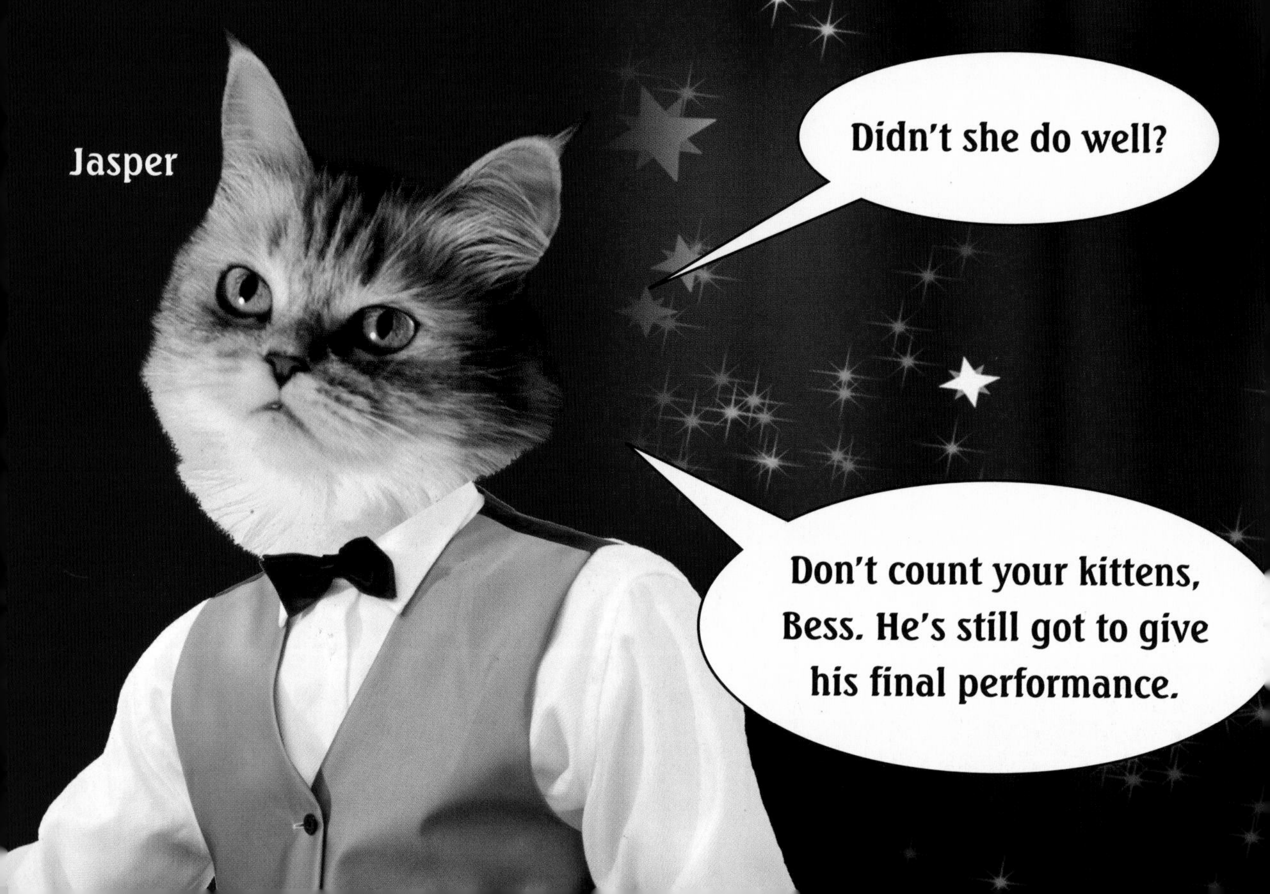

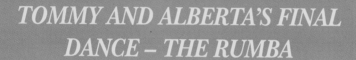

TOMMY AND ALBERTA'S FINAL DANCE – THE RUMBA

Catnipped Alberta can't control her kitten heels!

THE JUDGES' REACTION

The judges have never seen such catty chaos!

Bess

They certainly seem to have caused friction with the audience. Judges, what's the verdict?

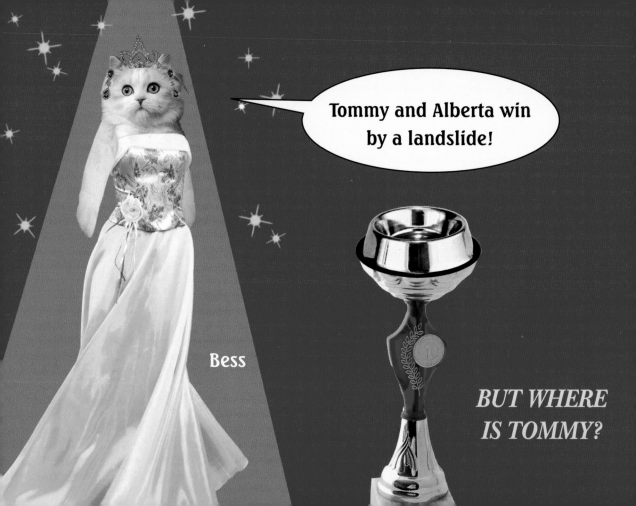

SACRÉ BLEU! TOMMY HAS ELOPED WITH NIGEL! DANCING HAS OPENED HIS HEART TO NEW, INNER LONGINGS. DON'T TELL HIS FAN CLUB – THEY'LL BE CRESTFALLEN.

STRICTLY CAT DANCING – LIVE TOUR!

For twelve weeks only, *Strictly Cat Dancing* brings you... *Strictly Cat Dancing Live!* All the dancing and glamour of the TV show, but in a massive arena!

• Witness the show-stopping routines and meet the cast from the original programme
• Heckle the judges as they deliver their verdict
• Vote for your favourite cat dancers and ensure they win the Golden Fur Ball trophy

You'll be close enough to see the fur fly!

'The costumes! The routines! The smell of thousands of incontinent elderly lady-cats all clamouring for a better look! Enough to make the fur stand on end. Riveting' **FELINE FRIEND**

'It's just like watching the telly, except the judges and contestants are really tiny and you can't see anything if the cat in front has a perm' **PAWS FOR THOUGHT**

'I took the mother, and ended up spending a mint on programmes and light-up wandy things. She seemed to like it though' **THE DAILY PURR**

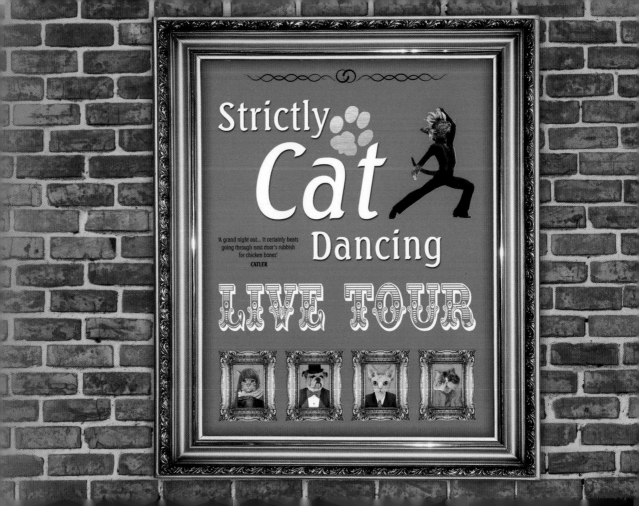

PHOTO CREDITS

Have you enjoyed this book? If so, why not write a review on your favourite website?

Thanks very much for buying this Summersdale book.

www.summersdale.com